A MASS MOVEMENT AGAINST DEMOCRACY
The Threat of the Sangh Parivar

A MASS MOVEMENT AGAINST DEMOCRACY
The Threat of the Sangh Parivar

Shankar Gopalakrishnan

AAKAR
In Association with
ŚRUTI
Society for Rural Urban & Tribal Initiative

A Mass Movement Against Democracy
by Shankar Gopalakrishnan

First Published, 2009

ISBN 978-81-89833-90-9

Published by
AAKAR BOOKS
28 E Pocket IV, Mayur Vihar Phase I, Delhi-110 091
Phone : 011-2279 5505 Telefax : 011-2279 5641
aakarbooks@gmail.com; www.aakarbooks.com

In association with
SRUTI
Q-1, Hauz Khas Enclave, New Delhi-110 016
Web : www.sruti.org.in
E-mail : sruti@vsnl.com

Printed at
Arpit Printographers, Delhi-110 032
E-mail : arpitprinto@yahoo.com
Ph. : 9350809192

TABLE OF CONTENTS

PREFACE
The Propaganda of the Sangh Parivar

Since the 1980's, a shadow has darkened India's polity and threatened the fundamentals of its social and political existence. This is the Hindutva movement, organized, led and driven by the Rashtriya Swayamsevak Sangh and its front organizations – the Sangh Parivar.

To most of us, this growth of Hindutva has been most identified with its hate politics - the killing of tens of thousands in genocidal pogroms, systematic stoking of hatred against Muslims and Christians, building on people's communal prejudices etc. But is this all there is to the Sangh Parivar?

What, in fact, are the Sangh Parivar's actual goals? If the only goal of these groups is to create communal hatred, why have they been able to build such large scale mass support in the last few decades? What has changed in these years that has created this political phenomenon?

When these questions are explored, we begin to find that the Sangh Parivar is much more than just a group of anti-minority organisations. In fact, it is perhaps the biggest threat to popular struggle and social justice in India today. The more powerful these organisations become, the less and less political space there will be for people's struggles. And hence we must fight these groups – not for the sake of secularism alone, not for the sake of our fellow minority citizens alone, but because otherwise the struggle for freedom, justice and democracy in our country may be set back by generations.

This booklet seeks to explore these issues. It will not aim to address the myths that the Sangh Parivar spreads about minorities, since there is already material available on this. For reference, however, a brief summary is provided in this preface, together with basic responses that may be useful in countering their propaganda.

Myths and Facts

Myth: "Not all Muslims may be terrorists, but all terrorists are Muslims."

Even if we accept the government's definition of who is a terrorist, this is entirely untrue. In India, less than a third of the organisations banned as "terrorist" are Muslim organisations. Internationally, the group that has engaged in the most suicide bombings in the world is the LTTE in Sri Lanka – a militantly atheist group whose members are mostly of Hindu and Christian origin. As of October 2008, according to official figures, two thirds of the people who have died in 2008 due to "terrorism" died in attacks by Maoists and Northeastern militants (1225 out of 1855). These are all non-Muslim organisations, and the largest Northeastern organisation (ULFA) has a mostly Hindu leadership.

Besides, the definition of "terrorism" that the government uses is contradictory. A bomb blast in a market in Delhi is "terrorism", but, until the Malegaon blasts of 2008, both the media and the government ignored repeated bomb blasts that were linked to the Bajrang Dal. Similarly, the planned slaughter of almost two hundred people in Mumbai is considered "terrorism", but the planned slaughter of 65 people and the driving of thousands from their homes in Orissa in August 2008 is not. Indeed, the massacre of more than 2,000 people in Gujarat in 2002 is also not seen as "terrorism." A commission headed by a former Chief Justice of the Supreme Court said that more than six months of "systematic pre-planning and preparations" took place before the massacres in Gujarat. In almost every riot in the past twenty years, more than 80% of those killed have been

Muslim, and in almost every case the official enquiries have identified the RSS and the Sangh Parivar as involved in planning the riots. Is this not terrorism?

If one uses a proper definition, we find that there are organisations in every community that have engaged in "terrorist" violence at some point. Terrorism and the killing of innocent people has nothing to do with any one community.

Myth: "The government favours Muslims and pampers them."

On the contrary, official data indicates systematic discrimination against Muslims. The Sachar Committee found that availability of bus stops, roads, bank branches etc. is lower in Muslim majority areas, even when compared to nearby villages with a Hindu majority. Muslims on average received only 2/3 the loan amounts disbursed to other minorities. The proportion of Muslims living in pucca houses is lower than the general population, both in cities and in villages, even if compared to others at their level of poverty. Muslims form less than 3% of the IAS officers and 4% of IPS officers, even though their population is about 11% of the total. Overall, the Sachar Committee concluded that on average Muslims are at roughly the same socioeconomic level as Dalits and adivasis.

Myth: "The Muslim population is increasing faster than the Hindu population, especially because Muslim men can have many wives. Their aim is to become the majority."

The National Family Health Survey has found that young Muslim women have the same fertility rate as young Hindu women of the same economic level. The higher growth rate for Muslims overall is due to the fact that on average Muslims are poorer than Hindus, and the difference is only 0.8% per year. Moreover, as per the 2001 Census, the rate of growth of the Muslim population is falling faster than that of Hindus.

According to the last data available (the 1981 Census),

the population growth rate of Hindus in Jammu and Kashmir is twice as high as that of Muslims, mainly because Hindus were and are less well off than Muslims there. The State of Kerala – where Muslims are more than 25% of the population – has the lowest population growth rates of any State in the country.

Finally, available data has found that approximately 5.73% of Muslim men have multiple wives – but approximately 5.8% of Hindu men do too. Besides, since there are roughly the same number of men and women, having more than one wife does not mean more children overall; it only means that some other man in that community will not have a wife.

Myth: "Muslim and Christian cultures are foreign to India."

Would you like an India with no biryani, no salwar kameez, no kurtas, no Taj Mahal, no Red Fort, no dupattas, no ghazals, no cricket? How about an India with no chillies, which were first brought to India by the Portuguese in the 16th century? All these things were brought in by Muslims or Christians, but everyone now thinks of them as Indian. Just because someone says these things are not 'Hindu', do they stop being Indian?

Myth: "Muslims got 'their' country when Pakistan was created, now they should leave 'our' country."

The first active political leaders to talk of separate countries for Muslims and Hindus were those who would later be part of the Hindu Mahasabha. Bhai Paramanand, later president of the Mahasabha, demanded this in 1905. At that time, there was no Muslim League and Mohammad Ali Jinnah was part of the Congress. Jinnah and the Muslim League did not change their minds until 1940, thirty five years later. Even then, huge numbers of Muslims opposed the idea of Pakistan, including the biggest Islamic religious school in India – the Deoband seminary – and President of the Congress party, Maulana Azad, who was one of India's greatest freedom fighters. The demand for Pakistan was a demand by a political party, not a demand by Muslims as a whole.

Since then, many of India's greatest artists and leaders have been Muslims. Some of our most famous musicians are Muslims; so are our most famous actors. Some of our best cricket players, Zaher Khan, Mohammed Kaif, Irfan Pathan etc., are Muslims. Three Presidents of India, Zakir Hussain, Fakhruddin Ali and APJ Abdul Kalam, have been Muslims. All of these people have worked for and loved India as their country, as have the other 120 million Muslims in India.

Myth: "The Muslims and Christians always start violence. Hindus only attack out of revenge."

Every violent group – not just Hindu organisations - always claims to be acting in 'revenge.' The September 11 attacks in the US were justified as "revenge" for the killing of lakhs of people in Iraq and Palestine by the US and Israel. After the demolition of the Babri Masjid, the Shiv Sena killed hundreds of Muslims in the Bombay riots. Then militants set off two bombs and killed 300 people (including some Muslims) to take 'revenge' for the killings. Then the Shiv Sena killed several hundred more Muslims, again in 'revenge.' If you believe the emails being sent before the Delhi and Ahmedabad bomb blasts in 2008, the blasts are "revenge" for police atrocities and the massacre of Muslims in Gujarat. In August 2008 Christians were being massacred in Orissa in "revenge" for the killing of a VHP leader. If the Christians formed a militia, should they be allowed to massacre Hindus in "revenge"?

In reality revenge is no excuse for attacking innocent men, women and children. How does it make sense to burn, rape and kill people for something that they had nothing to do with? If we accept this kind of "revenge", then every group can claim the right to kill innocent people.

Myth: "Christian organisations are seeking to convert all the Hindus to their religion."

The proportion of Christians in India's population has actually decreased from 2.6% in 1981, to 2.5% in 1991, and to 2.3% in 2001. Some Christian sects are seeking to convert people, but so are Hindu organisations (such as the international Hare Krishna sect), and both have the right to do so. The claim that Christians convert by "force" or by "fraud" has never been proved. Orissa and other States have laws that make conversion by force or by fraud criminal, but in most States (Orissa, for instance) there has not been a single case filed under those laws – leave alone any case being proven. In fact the only confirmed reports of conversion by force concern conversion by the VHP and the Bajrang Dal, which have been threatening Christians in many parts of the country to convert to Hinduism or be killed.

INTRODUCTION
Seeing the Sangh Parivar as a Political Movement

Given the kind of propaganda that they spread, there seems little doubt about the nature of the Sangh Parivar. Most critics have seen the Sangh's activities as a way of distracting oppressed sections, turning them against each other rather than against their exploiters. By playing on religious sentiments, we argue, the Sangh Parivar serves the interests of the ruling class and divides the people.

This is no doubt true, but it is not enough. In fact it leads us to a double political problem. On the one hand we *underestimate* the danger posed by the Sangh Parivar, believing that we can defeat them by encouraging people to focus on the "real issues" and livelihood struggles alone. On the other, we *overestimate* their power by assuming that the Sangh is just another reflection of the division of people into different communities, and hence it can never be defeated until all divisions between people are defeated. The net result is that we reduce ourselves to a position of political impotence, either ignoring the Sangh until it is too late or responding by trying to counter their lies – in effect trying to compete on their own ground.

But are Hindutva organizations essentially just a reflection of religious divisions? Is the threat facing us and democracy today purely about dividing workers through fake propaganda about their religious identities? In reality, while these are part of the Sangh's work, to see the Sangh Parivar as *only* this is to miss three crucial features of their politics and their political action.

The *first* of these is the fact that these groups have far larger political goals than eliminating minorities.

The *second* is that these organisations are not just "playing upon" pre-existing religious identities and sentiments. They are actively *building* new identities in which people equate being "Hindu" with certain political concepts that have nothing to do with Hindu faiths as such. The Sangh is not some automatic product of a "communal consciousness" among Hindus. It is a *political organisation* that has, for more than 80 years, actively aimed to create a certain identity and consciousness in India, an identity that it refers to as a "Hindu identity." The spread of Hindutva is the result of the Sangh's efforts, not the cause.

The *third* is that these organisations are mass political movements. This may seem an obvious statement, but we tend to ignore this when we dismiss them as simply a trick intended to divide people. The Sangh Parivar has a genuine and very large mass base, a significant part of which consists of Dalits, adivasis, workers, the urban poor and other segments of the oppressed classes. This mass base is not purely the result of repressive violence or deceptive illusions; it consists of active, conscious mass support. Understanding why this support exists is key to identifying the threat the Sangh really poses, and therefore also key to fighting them.

To understand the Sangh Parivar, in other words, we cannot simply reduce it to being either a natural expression of "Hindu identity" or an exercise in ruling class deceit. It is a political movement, fighting for political goals in the same manner that mass organizations and people's movements do.

The remainder of this booklet is divided into the following parts. Chapter 1 tries to understand the ideology of the Sangh Parivar from its own statements and texts. Chapter 2 provides a brief history of the origins of the RSS and, later, the other groups in the Sangh Parivar, up to the 1980's (when they became truly national political forces). Chapter 3 tries to understand why ruling class support for the Sangh Parivar began to increase sharply in the 1980's. Chapter 4 outlines some possible ways of understanding how the Sangh Parivar recruits its cadre and builds a mass base. Chapter 5 briefly discusses the consequences that the expansion of the Sangh Parivar has for people's struggles in India. Based on the earlier arguments, the Conclusion lays out possible strategies that people's organisations can use to fight the Sangh Parivar's growth.

CHAPTER 1
Understanding the Sangh's Ideology

As said above, most analyses of Hindutva begin with the Sangh's propaganda against minorities. However, consider a slightly different angle – not what the Sangh affiliates say about minorities, but what they say about themselves. How does this movement describe its own understanding of society, its own politics and its own vision? How does it see itself as a political actor? The answers are surprising.

First, let's consider the following quote from a training textbook for youth being hired as teachers in the *ekal vidyalayas*, the Vishwa Hindu Parishad's latest educational effort (see chapter 5). This quote appears on the back cover of a Marathi textbook titled *Sanskar Varga,* as a kind of oath to be taken by ekal vidyalaya teachers.

> We are not working for any specific religion or class but for the entire country. All countrymen are our brothers. All are children of Bharatmata and so long as this feeling is not present in everyone, we will not sit quiet. We will strive to make Bharatmata content and happy. Bharatmata will, like Durga, kill all evil; like Lakshmi, will bring in wealth; like Saraswati, will remove the darkness of superstition and ignorance. Everywhere she will spread the light of knowledge. From the Hindu Mahasagar to the Himalayas, we will spread these seven values throughout the country: unity, hard work, equality, prosperity, knowledge, happiness and peace.

There are many striking things in this passage, but for the

moment the most obvious is that there is no mention of Muslims, Christians or "foreigners." Indeed the oath explicitly claims that the Sangh Parivar is not working for "any specific religion or class."

Similarly, consider a quote from the book *Bunches of Thoughts*, a collection of writings by MS Golwalkar – the second sarsanghchalak of the RSS, commonly known within the Sangh Parivar as "Guruji." When describing "Hindu Rashtra", this is what he had to say:

> As far as the national tradition of this land is concerned, it never considers that with a change in the method of worship, an individual ceases to be the son of the soil and should be treated as an alien. Here, in this land, there can be no objection to God being called by any name whatever. Ingrained in this soil is love and respect for all faiths and religious beliefs. He cannot be a son of this soil at all who is intolerant of other faiths.

Once again, this does not fit with the common understanding of Hindutva. Indeed, supporters of the Sangh Parivar often quote precisely these kinds of texts as evidence that the organisation is only demanding "true secularism." The BJP encapsulates this supposed "secularism" in its slogan "justice for all, appeasement for none."

Is this just public posturing for the sake of acceptance, a cover up of the hate-filled and genocidal violence that the Sangh actually engages in? Are these texts just meant to be an eyewash?

Certainly, but that is only part of the truth. These quotes, especially the first, come from internal texts used in the Sangh's own training exercises. Indeed, this rhetoric about "harmony" and "unity" is found in practically all the writings of the Sangh's key intellectuals, from its founder RS Hedgewar, through Golwalkar and subsequent sarsanghchalaks, all the way to Atal Behari Vajpayee. Indeed, as we shall see below, these concepts are in fact at the core of Sangh ideology. It is precisely for that reason that that ideology is so much more dangerous than simple minority-bashing. To dismiss such statements as lies is to underestimate their true danger. Far from being just a "cover-up" of the anti-minority and anti-people politics of the Sangh, they are in fact at its root.

Understanding the Sangh's Notion of "Unity"

What does the Sangh actually mean when it says "unity"? Other sets of Hindutva texts are helpful with this. The first is by Deendayal Upadhyay, an RSS pracharak, former president of the Jana Sangh and one of the RSS' leading intellectuals. His ideological doctrine of "integral humanism" is today claimed by the BJP as its "guiding philosophy." Criticising the "West" for adopting "democracy, nationalism and socialism" as its three mutually contradictory principles, he claimed that the 'correct' approach would revolve around the following lines:

> The first characteristic of Bharatiya culture is that it looks upon life as an integrated whole. It has an integrated view point. To think of parts may be proper for a specialist but it is not useful from the practical standpoint... We do admit that there is diversity and plurality in life but we have always attempted to discover the unity behind them....
>
> Unity in diversity and the expression of unity in various forms has remained the central thought of Bharatiya culture. ... Conflict is not a sign of culture or nature: rather it is a symptom of their degradation.

From these statements we begin to get a sense of what "unity" and "harmony" for the Sangh Parivar means. This is then amplified by Upadhyay's subsequent statement in the same lecture:

> In our view society is self-born. Like an individual, society comes into existence in an organic way. People do not produce society. It is not a sort of club, or some joint stock company, or a registered co-operative society. In reality, society is an entity with its own "SELF", its own life; it is a sovereign being like an individual; it is an organic entity.

The implications are perhaps clearest when we then find what Upadhyay has to say about caste:

> Here too, there were castes, but we had never accepted, conflict between one caste and another as fundamental concept behind it. In our concept of four castes, they are thought of as analogous to the different limbs of Virat-purusha. It was suggested that from the head of the Virat-Purusha Bhrahmins were created, Kshatriyas from hands, Vaishyas from his abdomen and Shudras from legs. If we analyze this concept we are faced with the question whether there can arise any conflict among the head, arms. stomach and legs of the same Virat Purusha. If conflict is fundamental, the body cannot be maintained. There cannot be any conflict in the different parts of the same body. On the contrary "one man" prevails. These limbs are not only complementary to one another, but even further, there is individual unity. There is a complete identity of interest identity of belonging.

This analogy between the castes and the body is familiar. But what is new in Upadhyay's formulation is the notion that this applies not just to caste but to *all* social groupings. Society is one organic whole, one system in which each individual and each group has a particular function under one overall command.

In other words, the "unity" and "harmony" that the Sangh speaks of is very different from the understanding of those words in common language. Normally, we conceive of unity as a means to an end; working class unity as a means in the class struggle, for instance, or unity of the people in the fight against imperialism. But for the Sangh, unity is not a means - unity is the *end in itself*. Society is meant to be "unified", it should be "unified", and the failure to be unified is the source of all problems. Inequality, oppression and exploitation are not features of society; they are either fictions made up by the "enemies of society" or aberrations due to the lack of unity. In fact there is no injustice in society, and there is no need for social change. What is needed instead is "unity." Thus unity and harmony here do not mean mutual respect for human dignity. They mean overall subjugation to some higher command, to which all human activity is to be subordinated. The "unity" of which the Sangh speaks of is the unity of a machine, in which all human beings except the "leaders" are reduced to obedient servants.

The Sangh's Explanation for Social Conflict

The existing society clearly does not have this "unity"; it is not an "organic entity", it has no "self", and it is divided by countless conflicts, oppression and exploitation. The Sangh sees this "disunity" as being the result of two main causes.

The first cause is referred to in the oath of *ekal vidyalaya* teachers above: superstition, ignorance, confusion, or, as Golwalkar puts it, a "crisis of character." Persons have forgotten their history, been confused, lost their sense of unity and been misled. They have become "selfish", small and petty minded, and need to be "educated" in "dharma" and brought back to the correct understanding. Without this education they will continue to be disunited and to engage in conflicts.

The second cause cited by the Sangh is a familiar one: "outsiders". The Sangh believes that these "outsiders" have taken advantage of the 'crisis of character' in order to spread confusion and disunity. As Golwalkar says, "The utter lack of consciousness among our people of belonging to one country and one culture has made them a fertile field for any scheming foreigner to sow seeds of disruption." The "Bharatiya society" (or the "Hindu nation") has been misled, divided and fooled by these persons.

And who are these outsiders? Golwalkar responds succinctly in *Bunch of Thoughts*: Muslims, Christians, and Communists. Muslims and Christians are enemies of the nation because of their "divided loyalties", their allegiance to invaders, their efforts to divide and convert Hindus, etc. This logic is the familiar hate propaganda of the Sangh

Parivar mentioned in the Preface. But his understanding of "Communism" (by which he means all left forces) is more interesting:

> There are some who feel that the growth of Communism is inevitable so long as economic disparity persists. But the fact is, economic disparity is not the real cause for mutual hatred on which the Communists thrive. The idea of dignity of labour is not properly imbibed by our people. For example, a rikshawala who makes a daily earning of 3 to 4 rupees is addressed as a 'fellow' and a clerk getting but Rs. 60 a month is addressed as 'Babuji'. It is this disparity in outlook in all walks of our life which creates hatred. This is a recent perversion that has entered our life. In our philosophy, there is no distinction of high or low in one's karma, i.e., duty. Every work is the worship of the same Almighty in the form of society. This spirit has to be revived once again.

In addition to dismissing the entire issue of social inequality and injustice, what is striking about this quote is that it indicates once again the essence of the Hindutva approach to social conflict – and the fact that this has nothing whatsoever to do with being "Hindu" as a purely religious identity. Golwalkar's attack on Communism has nothing to do with Communism's approach to the Hindu religion. To him Communism is an enemy *simply and only because it "divides" people in its approach,* even though, as he himself admits, there is in fact a difference between a rickshaw puller and a clerk. To him, instead of fighting to change those social inequalities, the Sangh should simply impose "unity" and uphold the existing oppression of people (doing otherwise would be against "unity").

While the Hindutva political project is built around a "Hindu identity", what this series of quotes shows us is that hatred for minorities is not simply because they are "not Hindus." At its root, the entire political project of Hindutva cannot and must not accept that there is a possibility of genuine difference and conflict within "society." But there *is* conflict in society, and the only way that can be explained is to draw a line between "society" and the "outsiders" dividing it. *The logic of the politics is such that it cannot exist without an enemy.* But the crime of the Muslim or Christian is not to have a different faith, just as the crime of Communists is not that they oppose Hinduism. Hence the claims that the Sangh is "tolerant of all faiths." Rather, the crime of all such persons is that they have been chosen as the "others", those responsible for the "disunity" in Hindu society.

Hence the aim of massacring Muslims and Christians (and repressing "Communists") is not to assert Hindu supremacy. It is to unify the "Hindu nation" itself. Slaughtering minorities is a means to the end of a "unified" Hindu society. 'Outsiders' meanwhile have a clear choice: they can swear allegiance to Hindutva and thus join 'society', or they can retain their beliefs, thereby confirming their 'foreignness' and making them fit for destruction.

Social "Uplift"

Even if the Sangh crushes the outsiders, though, it still has to deal with the fact that there are oppressed segments – workers, Dalits, adivasis, etc. - within its "Hindu society." How does the Sangh deal with this reality? The Sangh's answer can be seen in the position taken by the Bharatiya Mazdoor Sangh, the Sangh Parivar's trade union arm, on this issue. Its documents state that "The National goal cannot be achieved if there exists any feeling of enmity. The B.M.S. therefore, has deprecated the theory of class conflict and emphasized that all the constituents should act and work in unison. This can be achieved by developing the concept of "family" in the industry."

Once again, the overarching key goal is that there should be no conflict. Instead, society is like a "family", where – the Sangh says - the upper castes and capitalist class should function like parents helping their "neglected brethren." The latter term is applied to all sections of the oppressed and the poor, but particularly to adivasis and Dalits, who are seen as "backward" and lacking in "national spirit." Thus, Golwalkar's formula for methods to respond to untouchability is:

> programmes like bhajans, keertans, festivals, recital of stories from Ramayana and Mahabharata could be arranged, where all Hindus would assemble in a spirit of common brotherhood submerging all such differences as 'touchable' and 'untouchable' in a current of pure dharmic devotion. Service projects to promote literacy, health, sports, etc., should also be undertaken. Modern techniques like the audio-visual appliances may also be usefully adopted. However, the central point of all these activities should be the appeal to the heart, the emphasis on the unifying and ennobling factors, and ignoring of differences.

As described in chapter 5, the VHP has followed precisely this formula. In short, the solution is "uplift" - charity by the powerful to the "weak", and by the rich to the poor. But above all the "central point" should be "ignoring of differences."

In their work among adivasis, this emerges very clearly. Every effort is made to deny that there is any difference between adivasi faiths and the Sangh Parivar's version of Hinduism. Adivasi gods are made out to be just different names for mainstream Hindu deities, and their cultural practices said to be the result of "backwardness and ignorance." The Sangh Parivar thus describes their work among adivasis as "giving them back their culture."

Thus the Hindutva approach to social difference and social conflict can be encapsulated in a two faced formula: uplift and education for those "inside" society, destruction and elimination for those outside it. Together, these two means are envisaged as resulting in the inhuman "unity" that Hindutva believes is the ideal society.

The Role of the Sangh

This gives rise to the final question: if this is the vision being preached for society, then what is the role of the Sangh itself? What is its purpose and how should it function? One might expect answers such as the following: to struggle against the forces it sees as the enemy, and to raise consciousness and awareness of what it sees as the problem of Hindu society.

The answer that the ekal vidyalaya training textbook gives, however, is somewhat different:

> The aim of the Sangh is to organise the entire Hindu society, and not just to have a Hindu organisation within the ambit of this society. Had it been the latter, then the Sangh too would have added one more number to the already existing thousands of creeds. Though started as an institution, the aim of the Sangh is to expand so extensively that each and every individual and traditional social institutions like family, caste, profession, educational and religious institutions etc., are all to be ultimately engulfed into its system. The goal before the Sangh is to have an organised Hindu society in which all its constituents and institutions function in harmony and co-ordination, just as in the body organs.

In this, the textbook is echoing the much older words of Golwalkar:

> The Sangh therefore has never entertained the idea of building an organisation as a distinct and separate unit within society. Right form its inception the Sangh has clearly marked out as its goal the moulding of the whole of society, and not merely any one part of it, into an organised entity.

The Sangh, in other words, does not aim to fight for a unified "Hindu nation" – the Sangh *will become* the unified "Hindu nation." The Sangh seeks not to change the state and political structures of society but to replace them. All existing institutions are to be absorbed into the Sangh or destroyed by it. It is the Sangh itself that embodies the ideals outlined above – the organic unity of a single body following a single purpose, "uplifting" its "weaker sections" while destroying its enemies.

But this also implies that, once again, the Sangh is less concerned with defending some pre-existing "Hindu traditions" as it is with producing a totally new one, one in which endorsement of the Sangh's politics eventually becomes the very definition of "Hindu".

The Sangh Parivar's Ideology in Summary

This brief exploration allows us to identify certain basic tenets of the Sangh's political ideology:

- The source of all "evil" in society is social division and conflict;
- There is no genuine conflict within society, only artificial divisions created by lack of awareness or outside interference, and there is therefore no legitimate collective existence except that of the "nation";
- The only legitimate categories are the "individual" (who should be a "good Hindu") and the nation, and anyone who promotes any other group or collective identity is an enemy of the nation;
- The only proper response to social differences is to "educate and uplift" individuals within the "nation" and to destroy those outside;
- The Sangh itself is the Hindu nation, and it will absorb all institutions into itself.

It bears repeating that these are *political* concepts aimed at a transformation of state, society and polity. These are the fundamental ideological concepts of the Sangh, and they have little direct connection with the Hindu religion (though they may resonate with it). Moreover, this lack of connection is not just ideological. It is a little known fact that display of any Hindu deities is forbidden in RSS shakhas – the only images that are displayed and worshipped are the photos of the first two sarsanghchalaks (Hedgewar and Golwalkar), the *bhagwa dhwaj* and a picture of "Bharat Mata." Moreover, the RSS' uniform itself (the khaki shorts and white shirt) is as distant as possible from the traditional Indian dress of any community. It was modeled on the British colonial police uniform.

But if the RSS is not fighting for the Hindu faith, what is it fighting for? The answer emerges if we return to their concept of "unity." A unity that denies all difference, that suppresses all conflict, and that seeks to convert all of society into a machine. In such a "unity", dissent is seen as evil; people's struggle is seen as evil; fighting for justice is seen as evil. In short, *to the Sangh the biggest evil is democracy itself.*

By "democracy" here one is not referring to elected government alone. One is referring to the whole concept of society being built around the dignity and freedom of human beings. The Sangh project's immediate victims are minorities. But for the Sangh, these genocides are only steps on the way to a much bigger project: the suppression of all human freedom. The Sangh aims to build the ultimate authoritarian society, where every person is just a gear in a machine controlled by the "leaders."

But this seems an impossible idea. In particular, why does any member of the oppressed classes support such a project? Why do people join an endeavour aimed at destroying their rights? This will be the question that will concern us for the rest of this booklet. But first, it may help clarify understanding of the Sangh if we consider the closest historical parallel to its activities: European fascism.

European Fascism

The term "fascism" is inspired by two regimes in particular: Nazi Germany (1933 - 1945) and Fascist Italy (1923 – 1943)[1]. When discussing these regimes, two points usually

---

1. While the term has been applied to other countries and regimes – such as Horthy in Hungary, Franco in Spain, Peron in Argentina – the use of the term in such contexts is frequently disputed.

come to mind: first, the horrific massacre of more than 12 million people and the wholesale genocide of the Jews by the Nazi regime, and, second, the brutal dictatorships exercised by the fascist parties and their supreme leaders, Hitler and Mussolini. But there was more to fascism than simply the combination of dictatorship with mass killing[2].

First, fascism in both Italy and Germany was a sociopolitical and economic system of control, not merely a killing machine. Second, it was a mass movement in these countries, and a significant portion of its mass support continued until it was eventually destroyed by defeat in the Second World War. In both these aspects the European fascists had similarities to the Sangh Parivar in India, though these apparent similarities also contain differences.

The Fascist Ideology

European fascism was a political project with a complex ideology. That ideology was summarised by Mussolini in his *The Doctrine of Fascism:*

> The State, as conceived and realized by Fascism, is a spiritual and ethical entity for securing the political, juridical, and economic organization of the nation, an organization which in its origin and growth is a manifestation of the spirit. The State guarantees the internal and external safety of the country, but it also safeguards and transmits the spirit of the people, elaborated down the ages in its language, its customs, its faith. The State is not only the present; it is also the past and above all the future. Transcending the individual's brief spell of life, the State stands for the immanent conscience of the nation. The forms in which it finds expression change, but the need for it remains. The State educates the citizens to civism, makes them aware of their mission, urges them to unity; its justice harmonizes their divergent interests; it transmits to future

2. Indeed, the Italian Fascists did not engage in genocide, though many oppositionists and socialists were killed.

generations the conquests of the mind in the fields of science, art, law, human solidarity; it leads men up from primitive tribal life to that highest manifestation of human power, imperial rule.

Replace the word 'State' with 'Sangh', and the resemblance is obvious[3].

During the actual fascist regimes, this overarching 'spiritual' vision was institutionalised by the formation of what is now known as a "corporatist" state. This does not refer to 'corporate' in its modern sense of a company, but to a form of state organisation where each segment of society is organised in a federation according to its social function, with the state then operating as the mediator and superior for all of these organisations. Thus, under the Nazis, there was a single trade union for all workers, an association of women, a youth association, etc., and almost all Germans were part of one or the other of these associations. The Nazi party (and the German state, from which it was indistinguishable), under the supreme leadership of Hitler, coordinated these various organisations. The entire system was organised on lines similar to that of the military, with commanding "leaders" at each level whose orders were carried out by those under them and eventually by the population. Any political or social group outside these organisations was ruthlessly crushed, especially if it was a workers' organisation or genuine trade union, or if it was formed by the persecuted communities.

Even as all of society was organised on these hierarchical lines, the Nazis and the Fascists set up vast secret police establishments that tracked "anti-national" activity and detained, tortured and killed anyone they believed was opposed to the government. The Nazis also created a huge

---

3. Of course, the fact that Mussolini eulogises the state is itself a major difference between the RSS and the Italian fascists, but the parallel remains.

system of slave labour camps and death camps, into which they sent those who they regarded as enemies of the nation and the "German race": Jews, Gypsies, homosexuals, mentally ill persons, and – after the war began - Poles, Russians, and other Slavic communities. As said above, it is estimated that more than 12 million people died in these camps.

In economic terms, the fascists claimed to believe in an ill-defined "third way" between socialism and capitalism. In practice this 'third way' varied a great deal, but it had two fundamentals. The first was large-scale state spending, especially on military production and infrastructure like roads and railways. The second was a close alliance between the state and big corporations, whereby the corporations agreed to produce the goods the state required and demanded, and in exchange received enormous subsidies, total freedom to exploit labour and easy access to resources. Big corporations were encouraged to form their own associations and cartels to control prices, and in most sectors of the economy a few companies had the monopoly. Prices and trade were tightly regulated by the government. The expansion of state spending and the enormous investment in military production ensured near full employment, reducing working class discontent considerably. In any case, workers were forbidden to strike and eventually even forbidden to leave their jobs without the permission of their employer. Resistance was treated as treason and its leaders sent to the death camps.

Thus, in large measure, the fascists achieved their goal of a society with no organisation except their own, no space for dissent or struggle, and no possibility of democracy. Their control was far deeper than a mere police state, for it rested to a significant degree on the cooperation and support extended by large sections of the people to the fascists – the kind of support that has led to the German people being called "Hitler's willing executioners."

Mass Support for Fascism

This reality of mass support remains both the most intriguing and the most terrifying aspect of fascism in Europe. Fascism in Europe emerged at a time of social conflict, when large parts of Europe were witnessing militant struggles by working class and socialist parties and the shadow of the Russian Revolution hung over capitalists and imperialists throughout the world. Both Germany and Italy had witnessed mass struggles by workers, including the 1918 revolution in Germany, and in both countries the workers' parties – the centrist Social Democrats and the Communists – were among the largest mass formations until the fascists came to power.

Fascism drew much of its initial support from the social class that Marxists describe as the "petty bourgeoisie", namely those who possess their own means of production but who also engage in labour themselves (such as shopkeepers, small producers, etc.). These sections were organised into the fascist parties, and some of their members – along with the urban lumpenproletariat - were mobilised into military-style organisations that engaged in violent actions against trade unions, leftist organisations, other political parties, etc., and in Germany against the Jews. This violence would be described in India today as "riots", and the resemblance is not accidental; the Nazi "Sturmabteilung" (storm troopers) and the Fascist Blackshirts had much the same structure and drew on the same social base as the Bajrang Dal. With the tacit connivance of the state before their own takeover of power, the fascists in both Italy and Germany established a reign of mob terror, crushing democratic forces in general and the left in particular. Big corporates and industrial houses, while not seeking to join the Nazis and the Fascists themselves, bankrolled the fascist parties and encouraged their actions.

Meanwhile, these parties also promised a new reign of peace and calm, while engaging in hate propaganda against

Communists and Jews, who they accused of creating "disorder" and being "anti-nationals". The fascists projected themselves as the parties of the "common people", defending social values, tradition and faith against both the "anti-nationals" and the inequality and 'materialism' produced by capitalism. They claimed to be the advocates of the "common welfare", including the welfare of the workers – Mussolini was himself an ex-Socialist, while the Nazi party's full name was *National Sozialistische Deutsche Arbeiter Partei* (National Socialist German Workers' Party). These ideas were not just preached or imposed by terror; the fascists also gradually built up a network of organisations across German and Italian society, infiltrating neighborhood associations, sports clubs, student groups and so on and bringing them within the fascist fold.

A more detailed discussion of the class base of fascism will be undertaken in chapter 5. But these tactics produced sufficient popular support for the fascists to take state power through mass action. Mussolini in Italy led a massive "March on Rome" in 1923 which ended with the fall of the Italian government and the Fascist takeover. Inspired by Mussolini's example, Hitler tried to do the same in the famous "beer hall putsch", but failed. Ten years later, in 1933, the Nazis won enough votes to come to power as part of a coalition government, and Hitler was appointed Chancellor (Prime Minister). Three months later, claiming a threat from a "Communist conspiracy", the government imposed a state of emergency, and the German Parliament passed a law empowering Hitler to make laws by decree. The resulting dictatorship lasted until Germany's defeat in the war in 1945.

After taking over state power, the economic policies pursued by the fascists – in particular large-scale state spending, the build up of the military and the gradual creation of a "war economy" - ensured economic 'growth' and also a rapid increase in employment. Unemployment and hyper-inflation had been serious problems in Germany and Italy before the fascist rise to power, and the near full employment provided by the Nazis and the Fascists greatly diminished discontent among the working class and closed the space for left mobilisation – which in any case had long since been crushed.

Parallels and Differences with the Sangh Parivar

The resemblances between the fascists and the Sangh are quite clear. The organisational structure and political tactics of the Sangh and the fascists is – as described in the next chapter - almost identical, in addition to the strong similarity between fascist genocides and the Sangh's use of mass killing. Historians have also pointed out that RSS leaders visited fascist Italy and were greatly inspired by what they saw; Golwalkar's admiration for Hitler is well known. It is for this reason that many use the term "fascist" to describe the Sangh and its activities, drawing an explicit parallel between the RSS and the Nazis in particular.

But critics of this comparison point out that there are significant differences as well, in particular regarding the attitude of the Sangh to state power (which, in contrast to the European fascists, the Sangh has never seen as its sole or even main goal) and the lack of a single 'supreme leader' in the Sangh Parivar. A more fundamental criticism is the fact that there is a vast difference between the nature and balance of social forces in India today and that in Europe between the World Wars. Mechanical comparisons between the historical trajectory of European fascism and the Sangh Parivar therefore may lead to misunderstandings of our current political situation.

How can these similarities and differences help us understand the Sangh Parivar more clearly? This question will form the backdrop to the remainder of this booklet.

CHAPTER 2
The Creation and Consolidation of the Sangh Parivar: The Early Years

The Rashtriya Swayamsevak Sangh was founded in 1925 by Dr. KB Hedgewar. A member of the Chitpavan Brahmin community and a resident of Nagpur, Hedgewar believed that Hindus were "under threat" in the wake of a clash between Muslims and Hindus in Nagpur. Only six or seven people attended that initial meeting, at which it was resolved to build an organisation to strengthen the "character" and "defence" of Hindus.

Hedgewar founded the RSS in part because of a disagreement with the other major Hindutvawadi of the time, V D Savarkar, who had coined the term "Hindutva" and founded the Hindu Mahasabha the year before. Hedgewar had been inspired by Savarkar's notion of Hindutva, which held that only those who regarded India as both their "mother land" and as their "holy land" could be considered Indians. As seen earlier, this had little to do with the actual religion of Hinduism, and Savarkar clearly had little patience with those who sought to equate Hindutva with Hinduism. His concept, he insisted, was political and about "nationalism", not about religion.

Hedgewar believed this was true, and agreed with Savarkar that Hindus had been "weakened" by the divisions of caste, language, differences in faith etc., and needed to be unified with a new consciousness of Hindutva. He also shared Savarkar's intense hatred of Muslims and the belief that both Muslims and Christians – but especially Muslims – were "foreigners" and enemies of the Hindu nation. But while the two thus agreed on all the essentials of the concept of Hindutva and that Muslims were to be regarded as both inferior and enemies of the nation, they differed on how to respond. Savarkar was more explicitly political and hence founded a political party, the Hindu Mahasabha. Hedgewar, on the other hand, believed that there was first a need to build a "cultural consciousness" of "unity", and that this should be done through careful building of discipline and intellectual leadership. The RSS was to be the instrument for this project.

The RSS held its first meeting on Dasara in 1925, attended by only a few people. Subsequently regular meetings were held in Nagpur, where the RSS created its trademark style of physical exercises, indoctrination through speeches and 'games' that propagated its ideology. Some became *pracharaks* and were involved in RSS work and discipline on a full time basis. RSS members took oath to serve the *bhagwa dhwaj* (designed after the flag of the Peshwa kings, former Brahmin rulers of the area). The RSS also at the time began its practice of recruiting adolescent young men and indoctrinating them even before they attained adulthood. Strong emphasis was placed on absolute obedience to the leader and to the organisation. Women were and still are barred from membership.

In 1926 RSS members participated in another Hindu-Muslim clash in Nagpur, and over the years that followed the organisation began to grow throughout what is now Maharashtra. In 1931, BS Moonje, a politician and Hedgewar's mentor, undertook a trip to fascist Italy and returned deeply impressed by the Fascist youth league's practice of weekly sports and indoctrination meetings, involving youth as young as six. The RSS had already begun moving on similar lines, and it is speculated that Moonje's trip consolidated this approach into what is still the RSS' main form of activity[4].

The Freedom Struggle and the RSS

By 1939, the RSS had approximately 500 active shakhas and 60,000 members, and had mostly developed the complex leadership structure and hierarchy that it has today. Yet its base remained substantially Maharashtrian and upper caste. In 1939 Hedgewar died and was succeeded as sarsanghchalak by MS Golwalkar, who – in contrast to his predecessor – was the first to give the RSS a detailed and written ideology.

The RSS' attitude to the freedom struggle offers the first indicator of its later politics. Though Hedgewar was imprisoned in 1921 for his participation in Congress activities, he refrained from such actions after the founding of the RSS, except for participating in the Jangal Satyagraha with the explicit aim of meeting others to draw them into the RSS. In 1930, Hedgewar directed his cadres that they could participate in Gandhi's salt satyagraha in their individual capacity if they wished, but the RSS would not join.

In 1943, the British Home Office said the RSS had kept itself within the "bounds of the law" and "refrained from joining the August 1942 disturbances." Those 'disturbances' were the Quit India movement. At the same time, Savarkar directed his Hindu Mahasabha cadre to stay in their government posts and ignore the boycott calls of the freedom movement. Indeed, just before the start of the Quit India movement, Shyama Prasad Mookerjee, also of the Mahasabha but later the first president of the Jan Sangh, wrote a letter to the British Governor of Bengal saying: "Let me now refer to the situation that may be created in the province as a result of any widespread movement launched by the Congress... Anybody, who during the war [World War II], plans to stir up mass feelings, resulting in internal

---

4. See Casolari, Maria.

disturbances... must be resisted by any Government that may function..."

This is a telling revelation that belies this organisation's claim to be "nationalist." As has been pointed out by many, the Hindutva organisations were more concerned with attacking Muslims than with India's freedom. Moreover, the RSS has always had been very reluctant to confront state power. Historically, unlike either leftist organisations or their counterparts among the Muslim right wing, the Sangh has shown a remarkable tendency to collapse when faced with either state action or a concerted political opposition. As we shall see in Chapter 5, this reflects both the class character of RSS organising and the specific ideological and material basis for these organisations, and also offers a clue as to how they can be fought.

Despite staying out of the freedom struggle, the RSS continued to expand its base inside India. During Partition the RSS played a significant role in fomenting violence and organising the massacres of Muslims in Punjab. Shortly afterwards, ex-RSS member Nathuram Godse assassinated Gandhi; though Golwalkar was acquitted of a direct role in the conspiracy, the Justice Kapur Commission and other evidence strongly pointed to RSS involvement in the killing. As a result the Sangh was banned for a year. The ban was only lifted after Golwalkar accepted Nehru's condition that the Sangh adopt an internal constitution swearing respect for secularism and abjuring violence[5].

Despite its substantial spread in western and northern India, however, at Independence the RSS remained very limited in its social base. A 1947 internal Congress report on the RSS stated the following:

> The RSS has been a purely Maharashtrian brahmin organisation. The non-brahmin Maharashtrians who

---

5. Sangh supporters frequently claim that this ban was lifted due to intervention by the Supreme Court, but this is untrue.

> constitute the bulk of C P [Central Provinces] and Maharashtra have no sympathy with it... Even in the other provinces the chief organisers and whole-time workers will be found to be inevitably Maharashtrian brahmins.

Heavily dominated by upper castes, with no mass presence, it was essentially a marginal presence in politics even in its home areas.

Post Independence: the Sangh Parivar is Formed

Increasingly aware of these limitations, very soon after independence the Sangh initiated a strategy that would allow it to break out of these barriers. In keeping with its ideological goal of organising all of "Hindu" society, Sangh cadres were tasked with creating new front organisations for different sectors of society. Sangh pracharaks created new organisations for various sectors – the Akhil Bharatiya Vidyarthi Parishad (ABVP) for students in 1948, the Bharatiya Mazdoor Sangh in 1955 for workers, the Vanvasi Kalyan Ashram in 1952 for adivasis and so on. This marked the birth of the "Sangh Parivar"; the number of such front organisations now runs into hundreds.

Of these new front organisations, two were to play a particularly important role. In 1950, Shyama Prasad Mukherjee – a former leader of the now declining Hindu Mahasabha – founded the Bharatiya Jan Sangh. RSS cadres formed a key part of this new party and soon took over its functioning, despite Golwalkar's continuing claims that the RSS was 'apolitical.' The new party drew its mass base primarily from among small traders and petty industrialists; its politics reflected its base, with calls for greater "Hinduisation", removal of internal economic restrictions, and strict controls on imports.

The other important new front organisation was the VHP, founded in 1964. The VHP was explicitly aimed at becoming the "Catholic Church of Hinduism" - namely a single institution to bring together all varieties of Hinduism and all Hindu religious leaders. The VHP marked the Sangh's first venture into actual Hindu religious practice. The VHP also was the first in a series of institutions – the Vanvasi Kalyan Ashram was another – aimed at imitating what the Sangh perceived as the practice of Christian institutions.

In the wake of the founding of these institutions, the RSS itself retreated from direct involvement in public actions, and today the RSS hardly engages in any public protests or mobilisations of its own. It instead serves as the intellectual nucleus and leadership of the Sangh Parivar system.

Yet, despite the new base brought in by these mass organisations, the Sangh Parivar continued to be socially confined and was limited to some geographical areas. Its next breakthrough only occurred with the Emergency in 1975, when the RSS and many of the front organisations were banned (along with the Communists and the Jamaat-i-Islami). Once again, during this period, the RSS showed its cowardice in the face of state power by appealing for the ban on it to be lifted. Balasaheb Deoras, the sarsanghchalak of the RSS at the time, wrote to Indira Gandhi congratulating her on the upholding of her election (by a Supreme Court packed with her handpicked judges) and claiming that the RSS "had no connection" with any protests against the Emergency. Today the RSS claims just the opposite.

While the Sangh Parivar was by no means in the forefront of the anti-Emergency mobilisations, it gained a wider base as a result of joining the Janata Party, and the Janata government of 1977 – 1980 made several Jan Sangh leaders (such as Vajpayee) into Central government Ministers for the first time. The split in the Janata party \in 1980 was partly a result of the "dual membership" controversy, whereby the other Janata constituents demanded that the Jan Sangh leaders renounce their RSS affiliations. When they refused, the Sanghis split from the Janata Party, and in 1980 a new party – the BJP - was founded.

Shortly afterwards, the Sangh began a mass expansion that is almost unique in Indian political history. From a still small force in a geographically small area, capable of winning only two seats in the 1984 Lok Sabha elections, the Sangh Parivar grew into what was arguably India's largest organised political force by the 1990's. To understand this, we first need a broader framework of analysis.

CHAPTER 3
The Political Backdrop to the Rise of the Sangh Parivar in the 1980's

As mentioned in the Introduction, most of our analyses of Hindutva focus on the fact that it "divides" the working class. Yet it has been argued above that this is insufficient as an understanding. Where can one begin, then, for a different approach?

In the ideological debates during and after the time of the fascist regimes in Europe, both Marxist and non-Marxist theorists put forward various conceptions aimed at understanding these regimes and mass movements. The debate is still raging, and there is still dispute over how to characterise fascism as a political phenomenon.

The major Marxist theorists – such as Trotsky, Gramsci, Bauer and others - disagreed on the exact political nature of fascism, but agreed that it was a response of the bourgeoisie to the rising threat of a proletarian revolution. Trotsky, for instance, argued that fascism resulted from the rising despair and anger of the petty bourgeoisie (namely, the class of people who own some means of production but who also work and participate in production). This anger was harnessed by finance capital and the big bourgeoisie after the working class parties failed to develop a sufficiently revolutionary program. Capital in turn saw the need for such an action because it was their only hope for survival in the face of the growth and intensification of popular struggle against capitalism. In other words, fascism was an emergency measure, a desperate reaction by capital, and its mass support was provided by the despairing petty bourgeoisie looking for a political force that would defend them in the face of intensifying crises of production.

On this point, namely that fascism was a response to an impending crisis for capitalism, most Marxist theorists agreed. But on their face, such theories seem inapplicable to the Indian situation, where – despite widespread discontent and numerous local or regional resistances - neither the Indian state nor Indian capital are facing an imminent threat of revolutionary overthrow by any organised political force. This was even more true in the 1980's, when the Sangh Parivar began its historic expansion, than it is now. If one accepts that fascism is primarily a desperate response of a "capitalism in decline," Indian capital should have no reason to turn to fascism.

On this basis some have dismissed the relevance of this entire body of theory to understanding the Sangh Parivar. But there are some basic points that can be taken from these analyses, which might help us understand the Sangh Parivar better:

1. It is possible for a reactionary political project to benefit the ruling class bloc even though it initially draws its support from other sections of society (in the case of European fascism, the petty bourgeoisie).
2. Therefore, analyses of reactionary political formations should both seek to understand how they benefit the ruling class at that particular historical moment, *and*
3. Also seek to understand how these formations responded to concrete political needs among other sections.

In this chapter, we will postulate an answer to question 2, and in the next chapter to question 3.

Classes and Movements in the 1980's

Why is Hindutva a part of ruling class politics in India today? Exploring this requires seeing the changes that occurred in Indian politics during the period of Hindutva's mass expansion.

Like most societies in the world, Indian society is not strictly divisible into a class of "capitalist bourgeoisie" who own the means of production and a class of "workers" who do not own or have access to the means of production at all. A large part of Indian society – in fact the majority – consists of people who would fall "in between", though only if one adopts such a literal and technical understanding of class. These people own or access some means of production (such as marginal farmers, small traders, shopkeepers, vendors, etc.) but are either forced to also work as wage labourers or depend, despite their nominal "freedom", on larger capital for survival. In reality, they are indeed workers, but unlike the "assetless proletariat" they also have an interest in preserving and enhancing their access to the means of production. In most Marxist analyses, this class is the one referred to as the "petty bourgeoisie" or "petty commodity producers."

People from these sections form the vast majority of the support for people's movements and mass organizations in India today. Indeed, they are the core of almost all Indian political formations, forming the centre and politically active mass base of the left, centre and right.

Initially, in the 1950's and early 1960's, the Congress mostly provided an overarching framework for political mobilisation of these sections in mainland India (that is, excepting the Northeast and Kashmir). Yet as early as the 1967 elections (and earlier in the South), there were already signs that this 'unity' under the Congress was beginning to break up. The Emergency and the fall of Indira Gandhi in 1977 sealed the Congress' fate; it would never again be the "national" party. What followed the Congress, however, was not and still is not a takeover by some other single political formation. Instead, in the 1980's, India witnessed an explosion of mass mobilisation – the social movements, new regional parties, armed uprisings in several major areas of India's periphery (Kashmir, Assam, and Punjab) and eventually the Ayodhya and Mandal mobilisations.

Why did this happen? While the causes varied widely, the largest of the movements in the Indian mainland shared one characteristic: the dominant, or at least leading, presence of "rich peasant" groups. Zamindari abolition and the Green Revolution had contributed by the early 1980's to the creation of a small class of capitalist farmers and a larger, though less clearly defined, class of 'rich farmers' in most States in India (excepting the Northeast). These were social groups at the upper end of petty commodity production, often either having become fully capitalist or on the verge of doing so. These groups faced two primary problems in the 1980's. First, the gradual shift in terms of trade against agriculture meant that the value of their products – measured relative to industrial goods – fell steadily throughout this period. This threatened their ability to transition to capitalist agriculture, and in some cases even their ability to maintain their current conditions of existence. Second, the rise of these communities was not reflected in a concomitant change in political power, and they remained politically under-represented.

Simultaneously, other petty commodity producers were subject to an increasing squeeze on their ability to survive. In general such producers had increasingly become dependent on the market for survival, requiring them to also sell either their produce or their labour to survive. But at precisely this time, the government also responded to the demands of big companies and industrial capital, and began to allow them to penetrate into rural areas and to function with less regulation. The result was rapidly increasing pressure on smaller producers, both in urban and in rural areas.

This combined trend produced a shared interest across

the spectrum of petty commodity producers, which in turn led to the rich peasant-led movements of this period. These movements demanded that the state allocate more resources, subsidies, and other such supports to their forms of production (such as free power, fertilizer subsidies and higher procurement prices for farmers). While such demands mainly benefited the largest producers, they made sense even to the smaller producers, or indeed to any producer who sold any of their produce (such as any farmer who sold part of what they produced). The fact that these interests were shared across different levels of producers allowed them to be politically translated as the demands of the "community" as a whole – the linguistic community, the caste community, or the regional community, etc. As a result, across the 1980's, both parties and movements adopted the language of "communities" demanding state support, which became the political common sense of the 1980's. We can see this in the rise of regional parties like the TDP in Andhra Pradesh or the SP in UP, or in the "new farmers' movements" of Tikait and Sharad Joshi.

The Response of Capital

At the same time, the large capitalists in India were also changing their positions and politics. Until the 1970's, India's big bourgeoisie had built monopolistic large corporations through a close cooperation with the state bureaucracy, relying on state regulation to provide them with guaranteed markets for their products. But by the 1970's these companies also began to chafe at the state system, with the continued small size of their markets becoming an obstacle to their growth. State regulation also blocked them from easily absorbing smaller capitals and small commodity producers. The post-1980 Congress regime gradually began to change regulations in order to address these "problems". In 1985, for instance, the government promulgated a "New Economic Policy", with tax cuts, lower import duties, export tax breaks and relaxed licensing requirements.

Thus, at the same time as it came under intense pressure to grant increased subsidies and investment in favour of people mobilised in the various 1980's movements, the state also began to withdraw from regulation and taxation of big capital. The combined result was a sharp rise in state investment together with a 'boom' of consumer consumption (driven by the new availability of goods for the rich) and economic growth. Rural employment grew, agricultural real wages rose, and income poverty decreased at a more rapid rate than either before or since; it was an unusual period of "prosperity."

Yet this prosperity was built on a contradiction, for the interests of capital and the interests of the mass mobilisations were fundamentally opposed (though few of the 1980's movements were explicitly anti-capitalist). The demand for greater state support and assistance required state involvement and regulation, as well as allocation of economic resources through political decisions based on favouring "communities." But this was precisely what Indian capitalists, along with the now rapidly rising foreign capitalist presence, were opposed to. Capital was demanding freedom from all political constraints on their investment, withdrawal of the state from procurement and distribution, and the conversion of India into a unified market. State control over investment and state support for petty producers was exactly the opposite of what they wanted.

Throughout the 1980's the Indian state attempted to square this circle, with the result that the state descended deeper and deeper into debt as it both reduced corporate taxes and increased public investment. In 1991, NRI's and foreign financial institutions – the two main sources of finance for covering the increasing negative balance of state funds – pulled the plug by suddenly and rapidly withdrawing their funds. The resulting financial crash became the excuse used by Manmohan Singh and the then Congress government to begin the process of liberalisation, with the consequences that we know today.

Even as the pressure from foreign and domestic capital intensified in the run to 1991, Indian capital also needed a political project that could effectively oppose and contain the "divisive" and collective politics promoted by the 1980's movements. It found that project in Hindutva, which, as we saw in Chapter 1, was ideologically and politically opposed to any notion of a "collective" except the single, total and Sangh-controlled "Hindu nation." In this sense the Hindutva project fit perfectly with what was being advocated by Indian capital during this period – a unified "nation" and identity with no political mobilisation or politicised differences.

This increasing support was reflected in the rapidly changing attitude among the urban elite, who began financing and supporting the Sangh and the Ayodhya mobilisation in a major way. The BJP specifically targeted this elite segment and met with an increasing endorsement of its claim that the Ayodhya movement was not "communal" but aimed at making India into a "modern nation", a proud self-assertion against "sectional" and "vested" interests (meaning the other mobilisations of the time). From the viewpoint of capital, this was correct, for it would indeed help to create that truly "modern" vision: a single, de-collectivised unit with collective politics destroyed.

This support from urban elites translated into increased support from dominant social sections for the Hindutva mobilisation, reflected in growing endorsement by the English media, financial support and a rapid increase in the number of "respectable faces" (bureaucrats, military officers, journalists, etc.) who openly declared their support for it. But in itself this was not enough to convert the Sangh Parivar into a mass political force, though it was a necessary step in that direction. To understand the other half of this development – the growth in the Sangh's mass base – we need to look more closely at the functioning of the Sangh in this period and in the subsequent decades till the present day.

CHAPTER 4
The Individualist "Bargain" - The Sangh and Its Cadre Base From the 1980's Onwards

As the 1980's began and India's political landscape was increasingly dominated by turmoil, the Sangh Parivar gradually began to shift its strategy. Until the Emergency the Parivar had operated primarily on the basis of recruitment, training and indoctrination, with the RSS remaining the most dominant arm of the Parivar. After the Emergency, this approach was changed, marking a new phase in the Sangh Parivar's operations.

On the surface, the difference between the new strategy and the old was clearly apparent: there was a shift to emphasis on political mobilisation on a large scale. Instead of focusing on organisational discipline and full politicisation, the aim shifted towards mass protests and mass actions – along with expanded recruitment of cadre from multiple sections of society. Thus, the Vishwa Hindu Parishad was "relaunched" between 1979 and 1981 as a mass mobilisation platform. The newly formed BJP – despite initially vacillating between hardline hate politics and vague notions of "Gandhian socialism" - also soon became a platform of mass action. Finally, in 1984, the most visible and brutal element of this new mass strategy was also created, namely the Bajrang Dal.

The visible evidence of the new approach emerged in 1983, with the Sangh's agitations around the mass conversion of Dalits to Islam in Meenakshipuram, Tamil Nadu, and the "Ekatmata Yatras" that took place the same year. By the time the Ayodhya agitation was launched, the Sangh had fully concretised this model and was building upon it to expand.

But who formed this new mass base? It appears that the Ayodhya movement found its strongest bases in urban areas, among the urban poor, and in small towns. Urban peripheries also saw strong participation, as well as some rural areas in Uttar Pradesh and Madhya Pradesh. However, it does not seem to have enjoyed a strong base in most rural areas. The organised working class in many urban areas supported the movement, but were not its leaders. Geographically the movement was most active in Maharashtra, Gujarat and the Hindi-speaking States, though it had support elsewhere as well.

The New Mass Base

This vague mapping throws up an interesting point: it appears that the Ayodhya movement mobilised precisely the social sectors that did not fully participate in the other 1980's movements. Yet these segments were also mostly composed of petty producers – such as vendors and unorganised sector traders and producers in urban areas and small towns; peasants on urban peripheries; and tribal and other small agriculturists in those rural areas that joined the movement. And this support base was not just limited to the Ayodhya movement; it is among these same groups that, to this day, the Sangh retains its strongest base.

How did the Sangh manage to reach these sections, which should have had little sympathy with Hindutva ideology? The answer appears to be the Sangh's large scale recruitment of cadre among these sections, cadre who then provide it with a frame for accessing these sections and mobilising them. For these cadre and for their supporters, what did the Sangh offer that the other mobilisations could not?

There is no single answer to this question, of course, but

there is a pattern to the answers that emerge. That pattern, we can hypothesise, is at the heart of the Sangh's political machine; and, if so, understanding it is crucial if we are to understand the expansion of these organisations.

The pattern is this: the Sangh Parivar offered (and offers) people a bargain. Those who join gained material and social benefits, involving an increased sense of social importance as well as greater material and physical security. But, in exchange, they had to give up all claims to any collectivity except the Sangh; all identities except as Hindu individuals; and all struggles for rights and freedoms except those dictated by the Sangh. In short, the Sangh will provide benefits to those who abandon all identities and all freedoms – except that of being an individual, isolated soldier of the Sangh.

We can get a clearer idea of this tactic by examining the Sangh's work among some social sections, especially those who should logically be most opposed to the Sangh and its ideology.

Offering a Bargain: Sangh Activities Among Adivasis

The first such segment is adivasis. Building a mass base among adivasis has perhaps been the most intense and coordinated Sangh Parivar effort in the last two decades. They have mostly succeeded, even though it would seem that the adivasis should be the one segment of society that would be least attracted by Hindutva ideology.

The Sangh Parivar's penetration into adivasi areas revolved initially around 'seva' activities such as school building, hostels and medical camps. This first began on a national scale in the 1960's, when the Vanvasi Kalyan Ashram began working in tribal areas, focusing on training adivasi youth for 'respectable' professions such as law, medicine or the bureaucracy. In the early and mid 1980's there was a rapid growth in the scale of these activities, reflecting the increased flow of funds into the Sangh's coffers and the new focus on mobilisation. More than eight hundred schools were opened by the VHP in 1983 alone, mostly in tribal areas.

The number of full time activists in the Vanvasi Kalyan Ashram increased by six times between 1978 and 1983.

Such activities offered adivasis a clear avenue to individual advancement and, more importantly, to a sense of being included in "respectable" sections of society. Yet at every stage this was premised on abandoning their own sense of culture, identity and politics, and they were required to fully merge into the Sangh and its reconstruction of adivasi identity (as "vanvasis" who need to be educated and "uplifted" to normal identity).

Seeing the success of these activities, in 1989 the Sangh formally decided that "seva" activities – primarily targeting adivasis and Dalits – would be among its major methods of expansion. A "seva vibhag" was set up within the Sangh and a senior pracharak deputed to head it. In the years that followed, this was to make a huge impact on the Sangh's presence in adivasi areas in particular.

Among the new activities is one that is now a major Sangh project, and possibly among its most important cadre building activities. This is the *ekal vidyalaya* scheme, supposedly aimed at creating informal, alternative schools for dropouts from the government schools in adivasi areas. As per the Sangh's official claims, there are 26,314 ekal vidyalayas in operation at the time of writing, but the actual number is likely to be far larger. In practice, in many areas the *ekal vidyalayas* do not function very well and it is rarely clear whether children attend continuously. But the real importance of these schools is not the schoolchildren; it is the teachers, or *acharyas*, as they are called. The acharyas are local educated adivasi youth. They are drawn in with the promise of a stable salary – Rs. 300 or Rs. 500 per month. As seen in the quotes given in section 1, their training appears to focus not just on Hindutva propaganda but on a "social service" orientation, and the youth are trained to believe that they are working for *gaon vikas*.

For their acharyas, hence, the ekal vidyalayas offer both a material gain in the form of a steady income, as well as the chance to earn social respect through the performance of 'social service.' Yet, in exchange, they are barred from participating in any political work (including mass organisations) and affiliation with any political party. The Vanvasi Kalyan Ashram or the VHP are, of course, not to be considered "political" in that sense; they are only acting in the "national interest."

This combination of forcible individualisation and depoliticisation, combined with material security, implies that the subsequent loyalty to the Sangh will become progressively stronger and stronger. To dissent from or leave the Sangh Parivar would mean loss of security and loss of social status. Moreover, the potential for other avenues of discovering one's dignity, through collective political action, are all barred – and one is faced with a choice of either being within the Sangh's ideological and personal universe or losing the very real benefits that it provides.

In short, ***even before any indoctrination with Hindutva ideology***, *the acharya has already effectively consented to the Sangh's basic principles: no collective identity except the Sangh itself; individual dignity is equivalent to obedience to the Sangh; and any move to assert an independent politics or an independent identity is to be a traitor to one's own interests.* The subsequent training in Hindutva ideological beliefs is, therefore, presumably an easy exercise – with the passage of time, the loyalty and receptiveness of the acharya would be increasingly assured.

Other Social Sectors

Similar methods have been used in targeting other sectors. Among Dalits, the Sangh provides access to public spaces and positions of leadership and power – though, in practice, Dalits are never permitted into the most powerful or key decision-making positions, being at most used as showpieces. As an example of creating new spaces for Dalits, the VHP planned to build 100 temples in Dalit areas of Tamil Nadu in the early 1980's; and throughout the decade, such temple building activities were to become a standard Sangh Parivar tactic, offering both local employment and a space for "charity" to those in need. Common meals and ceremonies with Dalits, in keeping with Golwalkar's formula quoted in the previous chapter, were also regular features of Sangh activity, and most of the new temples featured common eating halls. In the Ekatmata Yatras, Dalits were frequently asked to carry the "holy water" of the Ganga.

For individual Dalits, traditionally denied all access to public space and suffering an increasingly intense crunch of unemployment and economic deprivation, this was no doubt an empowering experience. Certain Sangh organisations – in particular the Bajrang Dal – also focused and still focus on recruiting Dalits into their ranks, making them into 'defenders' of the community. Dalits now form the majority of Bajrang Dal cadres in several States.

Very similar dynamics operated with respect to urban women, especially those of middle caste and lower middle class sections, who are also barred from public space and public activity – leave alone political participation. The Sangh specifically targeted such women, both through the general Sangh organisations and through the "women's wings" of the VHP and the RSS (the Durga Vahini and the Rashtriya Sevika Samiti respectively). Because of its affiliation with "respectable" social segments, upper castes and religious leaders, the Sangh offered a "safe" avenue of political action that permitted women to participate in politics without facing family opposition. The specific promotion of certain women sadhvis – Uma Bharati, Ritambara – also offered a sense that, within the protected confines of the Sangh, it was possible for women to aspire to political leadership as well.

Indeed, in urban areas in general, the situation of women and Dalits typifies the situation of a large number of 'floating' segments who have been marginalised from both political organisations and economic security. The young men of such social backgrounds form the "lumpen" elements that operate as the common foundation of political parties, mafias and religious organisations in these areas. For such persons, becoming a part of Sangh politics once again offers advantages: access to support from wealthier elements, as well as contact with those in more respectable positions. Finally, the gains from looting and extortion during riots – with total impunity, given the attitude of the police to Sangh outfits – should not be underestimated.

But, for all segments, it must be remembered that these gains are only one half of the bargain. The Sangh cracks down on any move to raise issues of oppression and exploitation of Dalits and women, for instance. When not targeting minorities, the Sangh's women's organisations focus on training their members in being "good mothers and good wives." Even when issues of pornography and sexual harassment were raised by the Rashtriya Sevika Samiti, it was done at a very low level, and portrayed as a disease introduced into Indian society by outsiders. Similarly, raising any issue of untouchability or oppression of Dalits is immediately repressed within the Sangh's organisations. Finally, such benefits are also conditional on support for the Sangh's overall political project, and on participation in the horrible violence unleashed by it on a regular basis.

The overall message is clear, as it is among adivasis: in exchange for abandoning collective identities and political struggle, one will receive certain limited social and material gains, gains that can be crucial to survival. Yet those gains will remain forever precarious, for they are dependent on staying with the Sangh and obeying its increasing demands. Disloyalty or dissent means not just expulsion, but loss of all that has been gained. And thus, far more than simply by invoking abstract Hindu identity, the Sangh ensures the loyalty of its cadres.

The Conditions That Make Sangh Organising Possible

For us to fight the Sangh, it is crucial to understand what makes this model of mass organising possible. There are a number of factors that play into enabling the Sangh's expansion, and which have been consciously orchestrated by it and its supporters. Some of these are as follows:

Access to Funds, Both Domestic and Foreign, and Other Support

The previous two sections noted how "seva" has formed a critical part of the Sangh Parivar's expansion activities. This "seva" requires huge amounts of funding. The most concrete reflection of the support provided by capital and dominant sections to the Sangh is the enormous resources that these sections supply to the Sangh Parivar organisations.

There are three primary sources of such funds. One is local dominant sections and urban elites in India. Thus, when expanding in Madhya Pradesh (particularly in what is now Chhattisgarh) in the 1980's, the VHP drew heavily on the support of former rajas and wealthy traders. Even today the Sangh receives large donations from the local trading class and from businessmen. Corporate groups rarely provide open donations, of course, but in several cases also provide support.

The second – which is not well known – is foreign funding. The RSS' ties with NRI's stretch back to the early years of the organisation, and there are strong Sangh affiliates in the UK and the USA. Among these affiliates are organisations whose specific purpose is fundraising, such as the India Development and Relief Fund in the US and Sewa International in the UK. These groups do not just raise funds from Hindutva sympathisers. They also raise donations from the general public in the name of the supposed 'development' and 'relief' work that Sangh affiliates are engaged in. They typically claim that the Sangh Parivar consists of "voluntary" organisations providing training, "alternative" education and disaster relief to the poor. A typical quote from Sewa International's fundraising material is as follows:

> "SEWA International is a non-governmental and non-sectarian voluntary organization, ever ready in lending a helping hand to the needy, offering all assistance to the unfortunate and underprivileged by helping them reconstruct their life..."

The amounts involved are not small. One study was able to trace more than Rs. 30 crores in donations from one of the UK groups alone to the RSS in Gujarat during 2001, in the name of "relief" for earthquake victims. The ekal vidyalayas are heavily funded from abroad, and there is even a separate NGO – the Ekal Vidyalaya Foundation – for this purpose alone. The Vanvasi Kalyan Ashram, similarly, has a fundraising wing of its own abroad (the Kalyan Ashram Trust).

The third avenue of funding is from the state. This became particularly entrenched during the NDA period, when the Central government supported an enormous expansion of ekal vidyalayas and other Sangh schools. Between 1996 and 2003, for instance, the number of schools run by Vidya Bharati grew from 6,000 to 26,000. As a Human Rights Watch report put it, these schools "receive government funds, use government buildings, take control of state schools, train state teachers and exert considerable influence over state education boards."

This is not just true of BJP-governed States or the NDA period. The Sangh Parivar has so successfully infiltrated the bureaucracy and portrayed itself as a "social service organisation" that much of this state support now continues regardless of the government in power. The best example is the Ministry of Tribal Affairs' list of "Established Voluntary Agencies", which have easier access to Central funds. Even near the end of UPA rule, every single one of these "agencies" is a Sangh affiliate.

But can such funding be stopped? Much of it can be, for ***most of the foreign funding and state support of the Sangh Parivar is actually illegal.*** The Foreign Contributions (Regulation) Act – FCRA – bars any organisation notified as a "political" organisation from receiving foreign funds. The RSS, VHP, ABVP and some other Sangh affiliates are indeed notified as political organisations under the Act. While the foreign money typically comes to India in some other group's name (Sewa Bharati, for instance, which is a registered RSS-controlled NGO), since these are affiliates of the RSS, the donations remain illegal. Similarly, state support to the Sangh organisations typically occurs in violation of applicable regulations, which would bar supporting groups promoting communal hatred or political goals. It was on this basis, for instance, that the Central Ministry for Human Resources Development cut off all support to Sangh organisations in 2005.

One key task before us, therefore, is to identify the Sangh affiliates that are receiving funds, show the political and communal connections of these outfits and demand an end to foreign and state funding. This would be a serious blow to the Sangh and its operations. The RSS, for instance, considers foreign funding so important that it filed defamation cases against a group who revealed how the US-based IDRF is channeling money to Sangh organisations in India. When the UK Charity Commissioner's office, under pressure from activists, initiated an investigation into the Sangh's fundraising in the UK, the RSS tried to use contacts with the British Prime Minister to get it stopped.

Social Legitimacy

In addition to funding, the Sangh also relies on a second, more intangible resource when providing benefits to those who join it. This is what we might loosely call "social legitimacy" – the sense of an organization consisting of "respectable" members of society, engaged in social service aimed at the national good. The Sangh has deliberately cultivated this image from its early days and maintains it strongly at the local level. It is this image that generates a sense of higher social status when joining the Sangh.

Part of this legitimacy is the result of systematic efforts

to court the media during the 1980's, a sector which is in any case dominated by upper caste Hindu men and was already mostly right wing in approach. Extensive work with journalists and the deliberate infiltration of RSS supporters into the media has played a great role in producing the almost total pro-saffron atmosphere in the media today, so that even "secular" and progressive outlets hesitate to describe the Sangh Parivar's crimes in the same terms that they apply to "terrorists" or Maoists. Takeover of television spaces was a part of this effort, and one study has in fact identified Doordarshan's serialization of the *Ramayana* in 1989 as a key facilitator of the rise of the Ayodhya movement.

Meanwhile, the urban elite had also begun to actively support the Sangh Parivar in the 1980's, due to the dynamics mentioned in the previous chapter. Since the mid 1980's this process of mutual alliance has seen the urban elite and the Sangh move closer and closer together in a relationship of mutual benefit.

The Sangh Parivar's "legitimacy" then serves multiple crucial functions – it creates a sense of social standing for cadres who wish to join, it makes it possible for elites and corporates to support the Sangh without open allegiance to its politics, and it allows for state support. Denting this legitimacy is therefore a key part of struggle against the Sangh at all levels.

Moreover, this kind of legitimacy is also key to the reason why mere counter-propaganda, or building our own alternative schools and alternative cultural actions, may not necessarily be enough to fight the Sangh. Until we succeed in achieving a revolutionary transformation of society, our initiatives will remain oppositional - "alternative", in short. Even where we dominate the area, we will still be perceived as an oppositional force. This means that whatever we do, we cannot respond to aspirations for social mobility and higher status within *existing* society. Indeed, no political project that is opposed to the ruling class could do so, because it is the ruling class that defines what is respectable.

But precisely because it is a right wing ruling class project, the Sangh Parivar can in fact do that. If we wish to counter the Sangh, we must fight their legitimacy, not merely attempt to create one of our own. Our alternatives may reduce the recruits available to the Sangh Parivar in our own areas, but outside those areas, our actions will not reduce their appeal.

Elimination of Other Organisations and Other Alternatives of Political Action

Despite that, however, this does not mean that the existence of people's organizations does not impact the Sangh's expansion. The aspirations that the Sangh seeks to address are precisely those – the need for material security and for a sense of self-respect – that are also the driving force of popular struggle. There is also no doubt that an active, vibrant political movement, in which collective struggle for a new society is taking place, is far more attractive than the limited and partial individual gains that the Sangh offers to its recruits. Moreover, the presence of such political processes shows how limited and illusory the Sangh's offers of gain actually are. This is one reason that Sangh recruitment has been historically much weaker in areas where there are strong popular movements.

However, this has two consequences. First, it provides a direct incentive – in addition to their overall political opposition to popular struggle - to the Sangh to try to crush all popular struggles in its areas, typically by labeling them as Communist or Christian conspiracies. The situation in Chhattisgarh is a good example. This is of course easier in BJP-ruled States, but not limited to them alone.

The second consequence may be more dangerous. Where popular struggles *fail* and leave behind a cadre of people who are politicised but frustrated, insecure and unable to take the political process forward, or when cadre leave an organisation because of a sense of frustration, such persons may be more attracted to the Sangh's appeal. They, in turn, benefit the Sangh far more than average persons, since they are already skilled in political organising and have a position of leadership in the community. Many Sangh leaders among Dalits and adivasis are in fact former activists of progressive or left organisations.

Absence of State Repression or Concerted Political Opposition

Linked to the need for social legitimacy is the fact that, since so much of the Sangh Parivar's appeal consists of individual benefits, the Sangh suffers greatly when it is faced with concerted State or political opposition. Its popular base lacks any collective consciousness beyond individuals seeking the sense of security and benefits that it provides; so if that security and benefits begin to diminish, it risks disintegration.

This is why, if one notes carefully, the Sangh Parivar never attempts to directly confront state power. Whenever any State institution initiates an actual effort to stop them, they flee very quickly. We have already seen how RSS leaders pleaded with the Central government to lift the bans on it. Every Sangh-created "riot" and mass killing ends as soon as the police decide to actually act. This is also why States like Bihar and West Bengal – where, for various reasons, ruling parties have decided not to allow Sangh mobilisations – suddenly witnessed "communal peace" after brutal mass killings earlier. Despite grave threats about thousands giving their lives for a Ram temple in Ayodhya, since 1992 neither the VHP nor any other Sangh Parivar outfit has ever taken any action except when they are reasonably sure that they will not face state opposition.

Similarly, in areas where strong popular movements or other political parties confront them, their expansion is greatly limited. In Kerala, despite constant effort, the BJP has never been able to win even a single MLA seat, in large part because the left parties there have for a long time taken a confrontational line towards the RSS. Where the Sangh Parivar cannot claim to be a "social service" organisation, it finds it very difficult to expand at all.

This provides reason to hope. It shows that the Sangh Parivar is far from being the invincible voice of the "Hindu community" that it claims to be. We need not be intimidated by its apparent size, for underneath lies a paper tiger that will turn tail and run if we can target them correctly. Indeed, perhaps the best example to remember is how the leaders of the Nazi Party – that huge political apparatus that once threatened to control the entire continent of Europe – spent their trials after World War II denouncing each other and competing to claim that they were never Nazis in the first place. Not a single one of them sought to defend the Nazi ideology. The flip side to hate politics is always cowardice.

CHAPTER 5
Consequences for People's Struggles

Given their methods of building a mass base, the implications of the Sangh Parivar's expansion are far greater than merely dividing the people and creating an atmosphere of communal tension. Rather, the growth of the Sangh makes it far more difficult to wage people's struggles for justice and dignity, even if there is no open communal tension. Some of the reasons for this are explored in this chapter.

Consequences for Local Organising

As noted in the previous chapter, the Sangh's strongest base is among the urban lower middle classes, the urban poor, urban peripheries, small towns, and now among adivasis. It is not an accident that all except the last of these social sectors are areas where the presence of mass organisations, left parties and democratic movements is weakest. This is due to the fact that, in these areas, collective organising and a sense of community have already been badly damaged by atomisation, alienation and migration. Moreover, the possibility of meaningful gains through collective organising in such contexts seems very dim and rare, and the traditional demands of people's organisations do not seem directly relevant. In such contexts, the Sangh offers individual benefits like greater security, a sense of social respect and support from more powerful social elements. Given the lack of alternatives, this is a powerful appeal.

We can see this in the example of the textile workers of Ahmedabad, who were organised into some of the strongest trade unions in the country. Such unions also played a part in opposing communal attacks – in the 1969 riots, the Majoor Mahajan Sangh, one of the largest unions, played a key part in maintaining peace. But starting from the early 1980's increased imports wiped out Ahmedabad's textile mills, throwing most of these workers out of their jobs and leaving them to survive as informal sector workers. The unions mostly collapsed, unable to fight this new development and no longer relevant to their workers' individual struggles to survive. The Sangh moved in to replace them, drawing former union cadre and workers into their organisations. The result is that textile workers were among the key participants in the mass killings of 2002.

As neoliberalism intensifies and more people are driven into migration and displacement, the number of persons in these kinds of situations will only increase. These segments will become increasingly difficult to organise in traditional mass movement approaches. The growth of the Sangh Parivar will in turn provide legitimacy to anti-democratic and anti-collective politics, including state repression, which will begin to have an increasing degree of popular support as the Sangh expands. Moreover, when the actual violence against minorities begins, the resulting spiral of hatred and fear makes it almost impossible to build a collective struggle about other issues.

Even among adivasis, these trends hold true. It has been a common experience among most organisations that it is increasingly difficult to appeal to the educated youth among adivasis (or for that matter in other communities as well). The demands and struggles of the organisations often do not seem to meet their aspirations, which often aim at upward social mobility. Yet this is precisely the aspirations that the Sangh caters to, and these are the youth who are targeted (for instance through the ekal vidyalaya scheme).

The political impact of drawing such youth into the

Sangh Parivar may eventually be far higher than is indicated by their numbers. Educated youth tend to be the nucleus of political organising in most adivasi and other areas, including of most mass organisations. If they are increasingly drawn into individualised, anti-democratic politics, the result will be a shrinkage of space for political action and expansion for people's organisations, as well as a ripple effect on the society in the area in general.

Generating an Anti-Democratic Political Atmosphere

The above trends feed into a larger phenomenon that is more dangerous. The Sangh Parivar already dominates much of the regional and national media and – frequently – also has the implicit or explicit support of the state. Their appeal to educated youth then becomes a key access to local political sentiment. The net result is that the Sangh becomes capable of controlling the overall political mood in a manner that mass organisations cannot. It is a measure of this control that they have been able to make issues such as "conversion" increasingly central to our entire national political discourse.

The result of this is not only that hate politics will spread. It also means that the ability to bring people's issues into political action will be increasingly limited, as the Sangh will increasingly control the political terrain and continuously impose its agendas on it. This is already visible in the ability of the Sangh Parivar to, for instance, provide popular legitimacy to brutal state repression in States like Chhattisgarh. Issues and political problems are framed in terms of the Sangh's anti-democratic ideology, making all resistance seem "anti-national." Such concepts – once limited to the state and its urban supporters – will become increasingly all-pervasive as the Sangh expands.

Connections With Globalisation

In chapter 3 it was argued that, during the 1980's, capital increasingly began to seek a single unified market and a withdrawal of the state from economic regulation. These were potential reasons why the Sangh's politics appealed to capital in this period.

However, if this was the case in the 1980's, it is far more the case now. In the 1980's, the contradictory moves of the state, aimed at appeasing both the mass mobilisations and the desire of big business, led to the 1991 crisis. This reflected a contest for power and a battle over the state's economic role during that period. Post 1991, however, this battle was decisively won by the most powerful segments of Indian and foreign capital, and in particular by finance capital. With the onset of liberalisation, the effort to withdraw the state, to oppose state participation and to crush any mass mobilisation on economic issues is not merely a temporary strategy – it has become an entire political project.

At such a time, there is a strong overlapping interest between the Sangh's political goals and those of capital. The result has been a 'negotiation' between their ideological projects. The Sangh has dropped all reference to 'swadeshi' from its program and adopting a totally pro-US and pro-multinational position. Indian capital and big business, as well as urban elite interests, have in turn effectively endorsed the Sangh program while paying lip service to "secularism." While the two may disagree over the damage to India's "image", and to business, from the mass violence of the Sangh, this is a small irritant that has no effect on their overall shared purpose.

On the one hand, the combination of state repression and the effects of globalisation will act to suppress mass resistance and drive more and more people into landlessness, migration and impoverishment. On the other, precisely these factors, combined with financial and institutional support from the state and capital, will ensure that the appeal of the Sangh's organising model will increase steadily. This will in turn operate to close off democratic space for mass organising in response.

The Autocratic State With People's Support

The best example of these dynamics at work is Gujarat. In this state, almost all mass organising – except to some extent among adivasis – has been eliminated, its leaders either suppressed or coopted into the Sangh. This has reached the point where practically every major opposition force in the State, including the Congress, is dominated by either current or former Sangh personnel. Simultaneously, as described above, neoliberalism has eroded the base for trade unions and pushed farmers into an intensifying crisis, which they are incapable of responding to except through the Sangh's channels. The overall results were visible in the 2007 elections, where the Congress sought – at least in public – to raise the same issues as dominated politics in the 1980's and which still dominate most politics in India: caste issues, farmers' distress, etc. The BJP rode back to power with a landslide, having effectively destroyed the opposition.

But Gujarat is not the only such state. In Orissa, for instance, the same process is underway, as the Sangh Parivar and state repression combine to wipe out mass resistance. Chattisgarh is another example. Indeed, both Orissa and Chhattisgarh have shown how repressive and brutal this alliance can be, since in these States the vast majority of the population is still engaging in small peasant production (unlike in Gujarat) and hence big capital first requires them to be dislodged from their lands. The most intense form of such action is the salwa judum, planned by the BJP and the Vanvasi Kalyan Ashram with the support of Congress leader Mahendra Karma and – most likely - of the capitalists in Chhattisgarh. Once again, the aim of the combination is the forceful repression of all dissent and all democratic organising, combined with the cooptation of leaders and discontented segments into the Sangh.

CONCLUSION
Strategies and a Way Forward

This finally leaves us with a question: how can one respond to this offensive? How can we counter the Sangh's expansion? Strategies are in any case being designed by mass organisations and left formations at all times. There are, however, a few pointers that the analysis given here may provide.

Problematic Strategic Positions

First, if this analysis is accurate, there are some frequently cited strategic assumptions that are incorrect. If adopted, these may lead us into strategic mistakes. Some of these positions are as follows:

"The Congress [or other political party] is as communal and as right wing as the BJP and hence both are equally dangerous."

The fact that the Congress and other parties are deeply reactionary and anti-minority can hardly be disputed. When saying that the Sangh is our immediate enemy, one is not saying that the Congress is "better", or in any sense "less" reactionary. But the essence of Sangh politics, it has been argued here, is not their attitude to minorities, nor even their economic and social policies. It is their political vision, role in respect of the current political situation, and organising model. Today the Sangh is the spearhead of reactionary politics in India; it is the most advanced section of the right wing. These factors combine to make the Sangh

Parivar far more dangerous and far more complex than a political party alone.

Equating the Congress or other political forces with the Sangh Parivar is, in essence, to make the same mistake as the German Communists of the 1930's – who equated the Social Democratic Party, which was anti-Communist and pro-capitalist, with the Nazis. It is to say that all right wing political forces are the same, ignoring the political and strategic differences between them. Trotsky criticised the German Communists with a statement that is as relevant to our situation as it was to the German one:

> When one of my enemies sets before me small daily portions of poison and the second, on the other hand, is about to shoot straight at me, then I will first knock the gun out of the hand of my second enemy, for this gives me an opportunity to get rid of my first enemy. But that does not at all mean that the poison is a "lesser evil" in comparison with the gun; [it only means that the latter must be fought first].

"The Christian institutions and Muslim leaders make it easier for the Sangh to spread by alienating people with their aggressive tactics. We should oppose both."

Once again, this would be to mistake anti-minority rhetoric for the Sangh's politics. The Sangh has been able to expand in many areas where no aggressive Christian or Muslim presence existed at all. For the Sangh's appeal to people to work, it is not necessary that there be any immediate sense of threat from religious minorities – it is only required that the Sangh's model of individual benefits should be attractive. Whether or not Christian or minority activities lead to anti-people results and perhaps local social tension is a different matter, and it may be worth opposing them for that reason. But opposing them is not required for fighting the Sangh, nor is it likely to improve the situation.

"The BJP will never be able to come to power on its own in India, and over time the Sangh Parivar will be marginalised as people come to see through them."

It may well be correct that the BJP will not be able to get a majority in power on its own, but the political influence of the Sangh Parivar is not and never has been merely about attaining state power. In this they differ from the Nazis and the Italian Fascists; the Sangh Parivar's project is much more about social and political change, with or without power, than it is about seizure of power alone. The expansion of the Sangh is easier under a BJP regime, but it is by no means impossible without the BJP in power – and the Sangh has so successfully twisted the Indian state's structures that it is able to flourish under most parties. Open Sangh violence may be less when the BJP is out of power, but violence is only a small part of their political project.

At a broader level, it is indeed true that the Sangh Parivar will never win the support of a majority of Indians, nor will it ever achieve its goals. Their political project is too internally contradictory, and, at a certain point, when the Sangh's contradictions become too severe, it will collapse. But we are a very long way from that point, and in any case - like classical European fascism - the danger of the Sangh Parivar is not that it will achieve an impossible victory, but rather the enormous destruction it will create in the process of trying. Before the Sangh reaches the point of internal collapse, it will have generated a politics and a climate that is so opposed to democratic politics that people's movements, social justice struggles and progressive forces will be repressed or destroyed. No doubt resistance will arise again, but in the interim the defeat that would have been suffered will set back struggles for justice by many years. This is the function of extreme reactionary political projects; and if this much is done, the Sangh would have achieved its historical function for capital, whatever it may actually believe its goal to be.

Strategies to Fight the Sangh

The analysis does, however, suggest certain broad strategies that can be used in fighting the Sangh Parivar at the regional and local levels. These are not meant to replace the actions already being undertaken to strengthen secularism and tolerance, but rather as additional strategies specifically targeting the Sangh Parivar. The principle is that the *growth of the Sangh Parivar must be fought at an organisational level – the aim should be not just to target its propaganda, but to prevent it expanding as an organisation.*

Some specific strategies include the following:

Actively approach Hindutva and the Sangh Parivar as a Threat to the Organisation

In most cases, discussion of Hindutva and the Sangh Parivar begins at the time when mass violence is occurring in our area. This is far too late, for at these times it is impossible to effectively intervene against Sangh activity. At most some localised firefighting can be done through fact finding missions and protests, but by the time the violence begins, the Sangh has effectively already won. Hence, the first step in our response to the Sangh can be to initiate continuous discussion and preparation on its activities within people's organizations and progressive forces.

First, this requires ideological training and conceptual discussion on what the Sangh Parivar means for democracy in the country.

Second, it should include mapping their work as an organisation, such as:

- Who are their leaders in the local area?
- Are they expanding, and if so where and how?
- What kind of training is being given to their cadre?
- Which social segments have been supporting them, from where and with what kind of support (funds, material, transport, etc.)?
- What kind of actions have been planned by them?
- How close are they to the police, the bureaucracy, etc. in the area?
- What is their relationship with religious sects and leaders?

Such mapping is made more difficult because it is often not possible to know who exactly is affiliated to the Sangh Parivar. Appendix I contains a list of known Sangh outfits, which may be helpful in such mapping. Otherwise, it is useful to watch the positions taken by other forces such as religious sects and social service organisations, and in particular to look for the Sangh Parivar style of rhetoric – emphasis on "harmony" and "social uplift"; talk about how we need to help our "poor brethren"; etc.

This kind of mapping is critical, because the manner in which the Sangh Parivar operates makes it very difficult to know or track their activities without a conscious effort to do so. This allows to grow and claim social legitimacy, and by the time their activities and intentions are revealed, they are entrenched in the public consciousness.

Aim to Prevent Cadre Recruitment by the Sangh Parivar

The Sangh targets particular segments for its recruitment – educated youth and those who are already, to a degree, politicised but who are not yet firmly part of any organisation. In some cases, as said earlier, dissatisfied second rung leaders of mass organisations have wound up in the Sangh Parivar.

Targeting such segments for organizing by people's movements, and for anti-Sangh political education, may therefore be helpful. If the Sangh is not able to acquire a cadre base, it will not be able to expand into the public mind. Cutting off access to cadre can be the easiest way to stop the Sangh, preventing their growth before they are able to take over the public space. The lack of access to cadre is, as mentioned earlier, one reason that the Sangh's presence is weakest where there are already vibrant mass organisations. This is true even where those organisations have not consciously sought to counter the Sangh Parivar, and it would be more so if one did so.

Attack the Organisation, Not the Ideology Alone

The Sangh Parivar's standard response to any criticism is that their opponents are "anti-Hindu." Critics often unwittingly make it easier for them to make this criticism by focusing our opposition on the Sangh's propaganda and trying to counter the myths they spread about Muslims and Christians. This is of course absolutely necessary, but it is not enough, for the expansion of the Sangh is not due to their propaganda alone.

The history of the RSS and the Sangh Parivar itself is less well known, and it may be useful to raise public awareness on those issues. The goals of the Sangh Parivar, the crimes they have committed, the lack of commitment to any genuine empowerment of people, and their stand during the freedom struggle may be useful aspects to focus on. If local Sangh leaders claim they have no connection to the larger organisation, they can be asked to condemn the Sangh and its history. They should also be asked how they intend to address people's livelihood issues or local problems. The aim here is to place the RSS and its brigade on the backfoot, to force them to defend themselves as *political organisations* rather than as *representatives of Hindus*.

De-Legitimise the Sangh Parivar

In earlier chapters, it was noted that social legitimacy is a crucial component of the appeal of the Sangh Parivar to people. Denying this legitimacy can hence greatly diminish their ability to recruit cadre. This requires strategies that can identify corruption, casteism and criminal aspects of the Sangh's activities. Publicity about their sources of funds, the amount of money they are raising in the name of their work, their association with political violence etc. can help damage the Sangh's image. The aim should be to remove the tag of "social service" which the Sangh uses as a shield for its growth.

A further strategy towards this end is to publicly oppose

Sangh events and actions: demonstrations outside their offices, public meetings demanding accountability from them, etc. These would preferably target the 'main' Sangh outfits, such as the VKA or the VHP. If done strategically and at the right moments, these may also contribute to the sense that the Sangh is "controversial" and thereby lead to a loss of 'respectability' that it enjoys.

At the Regional and National Levels, Deny Access to Funds, State Support

Coordinated action can also be undertaken at a wider level with the following aims:

1. Discrediting the Sangh's public image, exposing what it is doing in the name of "seva";
2. Identifying and stopping sources of funds to the Sangh Parivar, especially the illegal foreign fundraising and state support to these organisations;
3. Embarassing corporates, companies, etc. who are identified as donors to the Sangh Parivar;
4. Filing of police complaints, along with publicity, against local Sangh leaders.

The aim is both to deny the Sangh wider legitimacy and to hinder their access to the funds and state support which are so important to their cadre recruitment.

With such strategies, or with other actions aimed at hindering the Sangh's growth, it may be possible to prevent the Sangh expanding in areas of people's movements and into new parts of the country. It is only through such tactics, aimed at an open political confrontation with the Sangh, that we can hope to fight it.

It has been the aim of this booklet to argue that this confrontation is, in fact, one of the most crucial tasks before left and democratic organisations. The Sangh Parivar's growth in this country has been an incredible horror for the lakhs of people who have lost their homes and their families, the millions who have seen their lives destroyed by its hate politics. But it has also been a tragedy for progressive politics, a huge setback for the democratic space and human dignity that so many have fought for.

We cannot afford to ignore the Sangh any more. We cannot assume that it will collapse on its own, or that people will see through its lies. The situation has now reached the point where, if we are to fight globalisation, if we are to fight Indian capitalism, we must also fight the Sangh. It is a fight for the survival of democratic space in India, and it is a fight to open the doorway for future struggles for liberation. The space for struggle is closing; the gun is soon going to be pointing at our heads. It is up to us whether we fight back while there is still time.

APPENDIX I
Partial List of Sangh Parivar Organisations

Please note that this is not a complete list, as there are hundreds of groups affiliated to the Sangh Parivar and most will not be covered here. If there are local organisations that one suspects of affiliation, it is important to watch for two things:

- First, shared office space and cadre with one of the main Sangh Parivar groups (for instance many Sangh "seva" organisations use the offices of the RSS, VHP, ABVP or BJP); and
- Second, signs of Sangh ideology – references to "vanvasis" and "girijans", talk of "character building" and "moral education", attempts to impose vegetarianism, etc.

Core Sangh Parivar Organisations

Rashtriya Swayamsevak Sangh
Vishwa Hindu Parishad
Bharatiya Janata Party
Bajrang Dal
Akhil Bharatiya Vidyarthi Parishad
Bharatiya Mazdoor Sangh
Hindu Munnani (in Tamil Nadu)
Hindu Swayamsevak Sangh (abroad)

Organisations Targeting Adivasis

Vanvasi Kalyan Ashram / Akhil Bharatiya Vanvasi Kalyan Ashram
Vanvasi Kalyan Parishad
Vanbandhu Parishad / Friends of Tribal Society
Kalyan Ashram Trust
Girivasi Vanvasi Sewa Prakalp
G. Deshpande Vanvasi Vastigrah
Birsa Seva Prakalp

General "Seva" Organisations

Seva Bharati
Seva International
Bhookamp Pidit Sahayata Nidhi (in Gujarat)
Utkal Bipanna Sahayata Samiti (in Orissa)
Swami Vivekananda Rural Development Society (in Tamil Nadu)
Vikas Bharati
Bharat Vikas Parishad
Janseva Vidya Kendra
Sanskrit Bharati
Lok Kalyan Trust

Educational Organisations

Vidya Bharati
Ekal Vidyalaya Foundation
Sangh Parivar schools by the name of "Saraswati Shishu Mandirs", "Shishu Mandirs" etc.
Dr. Babasaheb Ambedkar Vaidyakiya Pratishthan
Bharatiya Shiksha Samiti
Balagokulam
Sookruti (in Orissa)

Women's Organisations

Rashtra Sevika Samiti (attached to RSS)
Durga Vahini (attached to VHP / Bajrang Dal)

BJP Women's Wing

Organisations Targeting Farmers

Bharatiya Kisan Sangh

Others

Swadeshi Jagran Manch
Samajik Samarashta Manch
National Medicos Organization
Smt. Misri Bai Kedia Charitable Trust
Yogakshema Trust
Bharat Kalyan Pratishthan
Sri Ram Gram Vikas Samiti
Yog Satsang Samiti
Vikasan Foundation